The HUNKER DOWN

2025 POETRY COLLECTION

by **Eric Nixon**

Cover image and design by Eric Nixon.

© 2026 by Eric Nixon

ISBN: 978-1-953522-02-3
BISAC: Poetry / American / General

All rights reserved. No part of this book may be copied, reproduced, stored in a retrieval system, or transmitted in any form or by any process without first obtaining written permission from the author; the exception being a reviewer who may quote brief passages with appropriate credit.

That being said, I'm pretty flexible with fully credited adaptations. Please contact me if you are considering adapting or remixing any works contained within this book.

All situations depicted in this book are products of the author's imagination and may not match any reality known to otherwise exist elsewhere.

Published by Double Yolk Press in Lenox, Massachusetts.
EricNixonAuthor@gmail.com
EricNixon.net

MUSICAL PLAYLIST

A few words about the music.

In the notes after most of the poems in this collection, is a line telling you about the music I was listening to when I wrote it.

I find that music is not only inspiring, but is intwined with the creative process. In the notes after each poem, I frequently write which song I was listening to when writing that poem. Sometimes the song inspired the poem (almost always the feel of the music and not the lyrics [I honestly don't know the lyrics to most of my favorite songs]), and sometimes the song was just playing in the background. While the song titles often seem like I chose a specific "fitting" song for that particular poem, I would like to say that is never the case. Any song that I happen to be listening to is 100% completely random and dictated by the shuffle feature on my music app. I almost always write to my "Poetry Mix" playlist.

Normally, I would have a link here going to my Spotify playlist for this year. I made the choice this year to ditch Spotify completely because of how poorly they pay musicians, and how one of the co-founders of Spotify invests his money into developing AI weapon systems. We all vote with our money, and I choose to not support that. So, after something like twelve years with Spotify, I made the switch to Apple Music. Here is the link to this year's playlist where I've compiled every song mentioned in this poetry collection. You can listen along to the songs that helped inspire my poetry (all 10+ hours of it).

https://music.apple.com/us/playlist/2025-poetry-collection/pl.u-NpXmmWVsEakla

I know that link is long and messy, especially for a physical book, sorry!

TABLE OF CONTENTS

<u>January</u> – 32 poems
A New Me
The Hunker Down
She Isn't Responsible
Perceived Belongings
Idiot Disguise
Anchor On My Back
Thinking Of The Clown
The System
Wispy On The Wild Wind
Re-Booting
The Next State
Thick Blankets And The Cats
Time Has A Way Of Spending Itself
The Hibernation Time
A Second Chance At Things
The Bad Days Have Returned
The Art Made Me Sad
The Obligation
The Skipper
Delete
Get It Out
Surviving Is A Political Act
We Try To Focus It
The Act Of Creation
My Short Notice
Appreciating The Time Left
Overwhelm
The Deeply Unsettling Winds
A Beneficiary Of Privilege
Is This The Start I Want?
The Familiar Seat
The Stapler

<u>February</u> – 12 poems
Exiting So Freely
Leaning In
Nightmarish
Long Forgotten Perfection
Write About Something Other Than
This Not That
One With The Universe Again
Starting At The Exit
Wanting To Do Bad Things
The Death Song
The Winter Equivalent
The Shiver Of Winter

<u>March</u> – 8 poems
Correctly Focused On This Shitty Car
Exposure
Celebrate
Only Speaks Of Brightness And Activity
The Carnivorous Intentions
Spring Cleaning
You're Not A Number
The Not Quite Two Months

<u>April</u> – 4 poems
I Am Doing This
Society's Canvas
Mid-April Snow
I'll Wait For The Bus That Charges

<u>May</u> – 6 poems
Everyone Can Stop
The Lamp Lifted
Trains About To Collide
Any Kind Of Lasting
The Fuckwit Mating Call

Until All The Seasons Blend

June – 24 poems
Often Stunningly So
Holding Us Down
Writer With A Capital W
It Was Truly Vegas
The Mere Mention
Be The Light
Every Possible Second You Can Afford To Give
Mahoney
Escalation
The Grayish Navy Is Just Enough
Inspired By The Uninspired
Everworse
A Whole New Perspective
I Think This Is The Way
Sparsest Parade
Raising A Collective Finger
The Wake Of Make
A Cat Stopping By
Cahoots
The Simpler Times
A Poet's Dozen
Closing The Loop
The Last Bridge
Obliterated

July – 12 poems
The Baby Bunny
Just Not Feeling It
Let The Little Things
An Interesting Circle Of Events
The Big Boom
Nineteen Listens
Inevitable Collapse
Someone Else's Job

That's Exactly What They're Good At
It's So Easy To Imagine
Tim Key
Pennies Flowing

<u>August</u> – 20 poems
Mauvais Français Est Bon
It Can Always Get Worse
The Volcano
Pivoting Slightly
The Noise
Monetized
Purposely Not Sharing
The Smiles Frozen
Vanishing Into The Ravenous Past
This Is It
If I Could Tell My Past Self One Thing
I Need To Fold This Bag Of Laundry
Dreaming Of A Place
Ascending
A Favorite
The Pungent Crispness
Did The Chair Topple?
Rise Above The Standard Couchiness
The Summer Is Over
Trying To Raise My Vibration

<u>September</u> – 4 poems
The Past Is Hungry
Trying To Drown Out Their Voices
Flourishes In Shadows
The Longing Twang

October – 8 poems
Sans Plans
Moving To My Moon Line
Concrete Steps
The Only Difference Is You
The Prize Pony
Post Something
Get Off Our Couches
The Burger King Crown

November – 10 poems
Incredibly Rich
Stretching The Mind
Filtered
The Calendar Blinks
Mostly Full Of Red Lights
Fast Forward
Their Charm
Just Knowing
Earworm
Gravy

December – 10 poems
All Banned
When The Weight
The Purpose Of The Year
Face-Forward
Icing Over
The Flames Of The Endgame
It Tastes Like Shapes
What We Are Capable Of
The Ceiling
The Beautiful Thing

2025 total: 150

JANUARY

A New Me

A new year
A new month
A new me
Supposedly
Or, at least,
That's what
They say
Despite the fact
That time
Doesn't really act
Like that
I'm still the same me
I was yesterday
And the same you
Just because we passed
An arbitrary human-made
Marker of time doesn't mean
Now everything is new
And everything is different
Because it's not
It's still the same everything
And, to be honest,
It's probably a little bit worse

                January 1, 2025
                Lenox, Massachusetts

Written while listening to "Sun of a Gun" by Oh Land.

January

The Hunker Down

The hunker down has begun
Lessening time spent
On news and social media
And instead focusing inwardly
To improve and make better
The one area I can control:
My own life and my home

Blocking out the bad
Making more of the good
Building up myself
Preparing for the day
When I can rise again

>   January 4, 2025
>   Lenox, Massachusetts

Written while listening to "Labyrinth" by Taylor Swift.

She Isn't Responsible

The phone rings
An older woman
On the other end
Says she knows
Her payment, due
On January first,
Should be sent out
But it's our fault
Our credit card
Processor charges
A three percent fee
So she won't use it
Leaving her just
One other option:
Mail a check
Which she is doing today
But she isn't responsible
For how terrible
The US Postal Service is
And that it's not her fault
She wants me to write down
That she spoke to me today
And she shouldn't be charged
Any late fees because
The Postal Service is awful
And that's her only choice
Because she thinks credit card fees
Are awful and terrible
And that I need to write down
That she spoke to me today
I was pleasant and nice
And could not wait
To get off the phone
Where I could not believe
That people actually think this way
That because they don't agree
With one aspect of something

January

That now removes all responsibility
On their part
When they are late
In doing a thing
They have to do
And have done
Several times a year
For decades
Despite acting like
Every part of this is brand new

        January 6, 2025
        Lenox, Massachusetts

The view from an office at a condo development.

Written while listening to "Feel The Pain" by Dinosaur Jr.

Perceived Belongings

When someone takes something
That doesn't belong to them
That's called theft
That's a crime
And they are imprisoned.
When world leaders to it
By invading a country
Or threatening to do it
It's somehow justified
Either by divine right
Or presidential whim
And no one blinks an eye
Or puts up a fight
To counter their sin

           January 7, 2025
           Lenox, Massachusetts

Today he said he would not rule out force in taking Greenland and taking the Panama Canal.

Written while listening to "Where The Sun Beats" by Blue Sky Black Death.

January

Idiot Disguise

If, the nightmare future
Ever (eventually) comes to fruition
And traffic stops
To check for papers
Becomes a normal thing
I should make sure I have
An idiot disguise
(Just in case)
By putting on a red hat
Combined with a
"Hail Hydra"
(Or something similar
 In an insipid, yokely way)
Will get me past any blockade
And hopefully, to safety
Somewhere far away from here
…unless they read my poetry
Haha, but that would mean
They would first have to read
So, I'm pretty safe, actually

> January 7, 2025
> Lenox, Massachusetts

Sigh. Now he wants to rename the Gulf Of Mexico to the "Gulf Of America."

Written while listening to "Outside" by Calvin Harris and Ellie Goulding.

Anchor On My Back

It's really hard to get excited
About a new year that's freshly here
When it's started off terribly
And a quick look at what's coming
Is like trying to go swimming
While someone drops an anchor
Directly on my back while expecting
Me to continue heading along
As if nothing was wrong

    January 7, 2025
    Lenox, Massachusetts

Written while listening to "Starfield" by The New Division.

January

Thinking Of The Clown

Frowns abound
When listening
To the news
And thinking
Of the clown

        January 7, 2025
        Lenox, Massachusetts

Written while listening to "Let It Burn" by Le Blonde.

The System

The only way out of the hole
The deeply drilled excavation
Is to muster a newfound sense
Of something like determination
To get past the newly built fence
While planning the evacuation
Because freedom isn't really free
When you're bound and gagged
By the billionaires' system
Of going along with the fascism

                January 7, 2025
                Lenox, Massachusetts

Written while listening to "Dim The Lights" by Wild Ones.

January

Wispy On The Wild Wind

The barely there
Light snow falling
Is more for effect
Than for anything
Resembling snow
Since it's wispy
On the wild wind
Flitting this way
And that and this
It's not building up
On the sidewalks
Just flying around
Doing its own thing

           January 8, 2025
           Lenox, Massachusetts

Written while listening to "Twinkle Twinkle" by Kettel.

Re-Booting

Packing up and picking up
And moving away from this place
Is a dream I like to sing
From time to time
Every few seconds
Despite it being so pretty
And being where I'm from
But in the end
None of that matters
When I feel pulled
And called to another place
Where a re-booting
Can be occurring
In much better conditions

                January 8, 2025
                Lenox, Massachusetts

Written while listening to "Get Me Away From Here, I'm Dying" by Belle and Sebastian.

January

The Next State

Hey Greenland
Hey Canada
Hey Panama
(Canal only)
You can be
The next state
In the "United" States
Just ask
Puerto Rico
American Samoa
Northern Mariana Islands
U.S. Virgin Islands
And, of course, Guam
How that's working out
Just as long as you
Don't want to vote
Or have a say
In anything
Listen to his promises
Of full statehood
And join us
Only to be
A territory
Exploited
With no say

        January 8, 2025
        Lenox, Massachusetts

Written while listening to "Age of Consent (New Order cover)" by Cayetana.

The Hunker Down

Thick Blankets And The Cats

The bitter cold days
Like today
Make you thankful
For modern conveniences
Such as
Heat on demand
Lights when you
Want and need them
Thick blankets
And the cats that
Collect on them

                January 8, 2025
                Lenox, Massachusetts

Written while listening to "Resonance" by Home.

January

Time Has A Way Of Spending Itself

Time has a way
Of spending itself
When you aren't
Focused or
Directly thinking
Or doing anything
I wish it would
Pause during
These times.
Just sitting there
Staring out the
Window blankly?
Click.
Time will stop
For this.
Lost in thought
About something
From a long time ago?
Click.
There you go.
Time's got your back
And will re-start
When you're ready
To resume living
In the present

    January 8, 2025
    Lenox, Massachusetts

Written while listening to "Where You Are" by Coquinio.

The Hibernation Time

With the weather
Too cold and windy
To do much of anything
It's like we should be
Deeply steeped in
The hibernation time
Like that sleepy time bear
Who does those tea adverts –
We should collect
Everything and everyone
Important and pull them all
Deeply under the covers
Where it's warm and cozy
And wake up in mid-March
When the rest of the world
Starts reviving from
The deeply cold winter
And then we can yawn
And get going on the year

                January 8, 2025
                Lenox, Massachusetts

Written while listening to "Anecdote" by Ambulance LTD.

January

A Second Chance At Things

Are the leaves
Spinning in the wind
Beyond happy
Frolicking, spinning,
Whipping around,
Racing across
The ice-packed snow
Enjoying a new life
In mid-January
A second chance at things.
The first time
Was just being pretty
And dropping down
But now, they can cut loose
And be their best leaf selves

          January 8, 2025
          Lenox, Massachusetts

Written while listening to "Lose My Mind" by Jai Wolf.

The Bad Days Have Returned

The bad days have returned
When avoidance of the news
Is once again a priority
As one of the only ways
To keep one's sanity

        January 21, 2025
        Lenox, Massachusetts

Written while listening to "Open Your Eyes" by STRFKR.

January

The Art Made Me Sad

The art made me sad
So I left
Making me even more sad
That I felt like
I had to leave

>January 21, 2025
>Lenox, Massachusetts

Last weekend we went to Mass MoCA and all of the new exhibits were weirdly sad. Things like a looping video of a boat on a beach on fire and a water fountain roped off and filled with brackish water. While I understand the artists are trying to bring attention to a bigger problem, it was just too much at the wrong time. The news gets more depressing by the day and after seeing a few exhibits like this, we ended up leaving.

Written while listening to "Hot Like Sauce" by Pretty Lights.

The Obligation

The obligation
Wears me down
Trying to do good
And be right
Is like pressing
My head hard
Against a belt sander
Until all that's left
Is the stumpy nub
Where my headache
Used to be

        January 21, 2025
        Lenox, Massachusetts

Written while listening to "Shake It Off (Taylor's Version)" by Taylor Swift.

January

The Skipper

I'm the skipper
Always pressing
Next and skipping
The song I'm listening
When it's not right
For the moment
I'm mired within

                January 21, 2025
                Lenox, Massachusetts

Written while listening to "Pursuit of Happiness" by Lissie.

Delete

Delete delete delete
Not quite perfect?
Delete!
Pretty good but don't know
Exactly what to do with it?
Delete!
Awesome, but can't be bothered?
Delete delete delete!
Wipe the slate clean
And start, re-start again!

                January 21, 2025
                Lenox, Massachusetts

Written while listening to "Opportune Moment" by The Sheila Divine.

January

Get It Out

Do you have
Something?
Get it out.
Do you want
To leave your mark?
Get it out.
Do you want
To make a difference?
Get it out.
Never hold it in.
Never mind the
Regressive haters.
Get it out.
Let your work
Inspire others
So they can also
Get it out.

    January 21, 2025
    Lenox, Massachusetts

Written while listening to "Low" by Cracker.

Surviving Is A Political Act

Sometimes
Much like
These times
Just living
And surviving
Is a political act

        January 26, 2025
        Lenox, Massachusetts

Written while listening to "Wedding Photo Stranger" by Matt Berry.

January

We Try To Focus It

The darkness
We all sometimes feel
Heavy
Dense
Dangerous
Gritty
Ugly
We try to ignore it
Or, we try to focus it
Inward or
Outward
Neither way
Is good for the
Subject, the
Target
Of the affection
The piles
Of feelings
Rank and
Dark
That can easily
Dump and
Smother
Or stab and
Puncture
Or everything
All at once
All over
Everyone
Who happens across
This happy scene

           January 26, 2025
           Lenox, Massachusetts

The Hunker Down

This is a great example of my "method writing." I'm in a delightful mood. Things are (mostly) going very well at the moment, and I don't feel like what I wrote in the slightest. However, this song came up in my Poetry playlist and holy wow, does it set the mood. I just wrote to the general gritty feeling of the song and got this.

Written while listening to "My Blood Runs Through This Land" by **Black Belt Eagle Scout**.

January

The Act Of Creation

The act of creation
Is a beautiful thing
The concept of
Bringing something
Out of nothing
Is truly amazing
And is even better
If it is a thing of beauty

        January 27, 2025
        Lenox, Massachusetts

Written while listening to "Simplicity Is Bliss" by Rufus du Sol.

My Short Notice

Working out
My short notice
Is more stressful
Than you'd assume
Since I actually care
About those who
Come after me
Making sure
They've got
What they need
So, I'm spending
All of my time
In these last days
Typing furiously
Building a guide
That helps explain
All of the things
I never knew and
I was never shown
And had to
Figure out
For myself
But now they'll have
This handy dandy guide
Helping them
Find their footing
When, for me,
There was none

                January 27, 2025
                Lenox, Massachusetts

Written while listening to "Take Away The Words" by Winterpills.

January

Appreciating The Time Left

Appreciating the time left
While I still have it
Here, within my grasp
The actually pretty view
And plenty of free time
To write and to think
When soon
I will have neither
As I go into something
That I know fully
And completely
And fully know
That my free time
From then onward
Will be nonexistent

        January 27, 2025
        Lenox, Massachusetts

Written while listening to "Mezzo" by The 77s.

Overwhelm

Despite me
Purposely avoiding
As much news as possible
Too much crap
Is seeping through
But, that's the point
They're trying to
Overwhelm and
Completely bury us
In too much, too fast
As a way to hopefully
Get as much past us
Without being noticed
As many are doing
What I'm doing
And trying to avoid
As much as possible

                January 27, 2025
                Lenox, Massachusetts

Written while listening to "Let's Make a Mistake Tonight" by Tennis.

January

The Deeply Unsettling Winds

The deeply unsettling winds
Continuously blowing when
The anticipation is building
As we all are knowing
Something bad is coming
So we all go inside
Hunkering down
Protecting what is important
Against the evil approaching

>January 28, 2025
>Lenox, Massachusetts

Written while listening to "Paradise Circus" by Massive Attack.

A Beneficiary Of Privilege

Just as long as you
Are a beneficiary
Of privilege
Based on your looks
Your upbringing
Or almost anything
That gave you
An advantage
And you don't need
Help or support
In any shape or form
Or are a recipient
Of a grant or money
Because none of that
Will ever be coming
It has been cancelled
And subsequently diverted
Into the pockets
Of the billionaires
Who apparently need it more

        January 28, 2025
        Lenox, Massachusetts

Written while listening to "Blue Jeans - RAC Mix" by Lana Del Rey and RAC.

January

Is This The Start I Want?

Is this the start I want?
One out of a dozen
Done and gone
I feel like I should be
More sure-footed
More on-track
Than the current
Off-kilter feeling
Like a pinball
Hitting and careening
All around amid
The confusing
Lights and sounds
Overwhelmed
While bouncing around
Wishing all of this
Would please stop

    January 28, 2025
    Lenox, Massachusetts

Written while listening to "Hold on to Your Friends" by Morrissey.

The Familiar Seat

The familiar seat
In the familiar place
Where I've been
For almost a year
That, soon,
In two days,
Will only exist
To me
In memories

    January 28, 2025
    Lee, Massachusetts

I'm leaving this job in two days. Will I miss it? A little.

Written while listening to "Gay Sons of Lesbian Mothers" by Kaki King.

The Stapler

Back in 2002
When I was not even thirty
At my work we ordered
A few new staplers
They were very modern
Rubberized plastic
Matte black and ergonomic
Designed to lie down
Or stand up on its front
Either way, they looked sleek
And were so easy to use
Already standing up
Just grab, squeeze
And your paper is stapled

In late 2005
When I left that workplace
I took my new stapler
Because I really liked it
And hadn't seen anything
As nice or modern since
So, as I moved around the country
So did this Swingline stapler
And every time I unpacked
All of my things, I unpacked
This stapler, putting it on my desk
Again and again
From New Hampshire
To Alabama
To Massachusetts
To another part of Massachusetts
To another part of Massachusetts
To Vermont
To Oregon
To Illinois
To Massachusetts
To Washington

The Hunker Down

To Massachusetts
And finally
To an actual house
In another part of Massachusetts
Each and every time
There was this little trooper
The steadfast office helper
Always ready to staple paper
The few times I year I needed that done
In my home office
But now
At this workplace
I'm leaving today
I had to buy a new stapler
And chose another Swingline
Solid steel, but sky blue in color
Mixed with the slightest gray
Making this a beautiful stapler
Which got me looking at
And thinking about
My trusty stapler
That's been with me
For nearly a quarter century
That, for some reason,
I brought to work
And swapped out with
The new blue stapler
Yes, partially because of the color
And partially due to it being new
That the new blue is more in-line
With my design aesthetic
So, with surprising sadness
Today I will be saying
A final goodbye to my stapler friend
And it's hitting me with difficulty
Thinking that I might have just
Stapled my last paper with it
A few minutes ago
And after I leave today

January

I will never see it again
For the rest of my life
And trusting that
The next person
Who works here
Replacing me
Will enjoy this stapler
As much as I did
And maybe they'll take it home
Just like I did
And give it new life
And new adventures
For another quarter century

        January 30, 2025
        Lee, Massachusetts

A whole lotta feels about a stupid stapler.

Written while listening to:
"Anthems for a Seventeen Year-Old Girl" by Broken Social Scene
"Clarity" by Hammock
"Hopopono" by GoGo Penguin
"Experience" by Ludovico Einaudi and Daniel Hope

The Hunker Down

FEBRUARY

Exiting So Freely

We all want room,
Space between
Us and that
Which is next to us
But life is like
A car park
Where the lines
Are entirely
Too close
To one another
Cramped tight
And so awkward
When trying
To exit gracefully
When all we really
Want is more room
Between the cars
Twice the space
So we can open
Our doors
Exiting
So freely
Without having
To be thinking
Or considering
All the others
All the time

        February 22, 2025
        Lenox, Massachusetts

Written while listening to "Zima" by Sultan + Shepard and Delhia De France.

Leaning In

The strength it takes
To avoid avoidance
To see the bubbling mess
Of pure emotion
And not be repulsed
Or scared, or be
Turning, running
But instead
To be the one
Leaning in
And holding close
Making contact
Offering comfort
When no one would

        February 22, 2025
        Lenox, Massachusetts

Written while listening to "Je suis le vent" by Working for a Nuclear Free City.

Nightmarish

This place
In this time
Seems more
Nightmarish
Every single
Day that passes
Feeling like
There can't
Be many more
Like this
(But there are)
Or feeling like
Soon it will all
Just end
For all of us

        February 22, 2025
        Lenox, Massachusetts

Written while listening to "Driver 8 (REM cover)" by Toad The Wet Sprocket, Robin Wilson, and Matt Scannell.

February

Long Forgotten Perfection

Listening to a song
I really like on Spotify
I tap the artist's name
The creator of this
Long forgotten bit
Of absolute perfection
And see, to my horror,
That this band only gets
42 listens a month
When it should get
A thousand times more
So, I do the right thing
When the song ends
And play it again
And again
And again

>February 22, 2025
>Lenox, Massachusetts

Written while listening to "The World's Best Ex Boyfriend" by Ad Frank.

This song is awesome.

The Hunker Down

Write About Something Other Than

These days
It takes
A little longer
A little more thought
And planning
To write about
Something
Other than
The horror
Descending
Destroying
The country
249 years
In the making

        February 22, 2025
        Lenox, Massachusetts

Written while listening to "Stayin' Alive" by Say Lou Lou.

This Not That

Sometimes I forget
During the spaces
The times in-between
When the poetry thing
Seems as distant as
Lasting peace
When I am deeply in
The paycheck work
When I finally sit
Down to the keyboard
With the intention
Of poetic expression
That this is what I do
And I should never
Let so much time
Slip by
Without doing
This writing thing
Because this,
Not that,
Is where I belong

    February 22, 2025
    Lenox, Massachusetts

Written while listening to "These Are The Fables" by The New Pornographers.

One With The Universe Again

Cancer
Ravenous
A great woman
Withered
The buoyant energy
Moored and floored
Stranded on the sand
All humanity removed
Until the last breath…

…and she is made whole,
No longer defined
By pain and disease,
Perfect and refreshed
In absolutely every way –
One with the Universe again

> February 22, 2025
> Lenox, Massachusetts

My aunt, Marge Nixon, passed away this evening.

Written while listening to "Utopia" by Digitalism.

Starting At The Exit

The journey
Starting at
The exit
Is so scary
And wonderful
And only
Gets better
The further
Removed
You are
From Earth

        February 22, 2025
        Lenox, Massachusetts

Written while listening to "All In A Dream" by LP Giobbi, DJ Tennis, and Joseph Ashworth.

Wanting To Do Bad Things

The wanting
To do bad things
Is diminishing
With time
As the connecting
With intuition
Is becoming
More secure

        February 22, 2025
        Lenox, Massachusetts

I was going to eat some Trader Joe's cookies, but I resisted.

Written while listening to "Sharing A Gibson with Martin Luther King Jr. (live)" by Lambchop.

February

The Death Song

Is this a sign?
An odd coincidence
When the same song
That strikes me hard
Because on the day
My father died
Twenty-one years ago
Driving home
This song came on
Hitting me deeply
And unexpectedly
And I've always
Secretly called this
"The death song"
Only in my mind
And here it is
Playing now
All on its own
Unprompted by me
But probably chosen
By the ghosts
Swirling about
As a way
To poke and prod
The emotions
Fueling the feelings
And the emotions
As the replaying
Of memories
Starts and doesn't stop
As her spirit
Gets the send-off
It deserves

February 22, 2025
Lenox, Massachusetts

The Hunker Down

Written while listening to "All At Once" by Pete Yorn.

Diggity dang, song. Why you got to do a thing?

Also, another really weird coincidence…this was the 42nd poem I wrote this year. Marge Nixon (my aunt who died tonight), was in room 42 for the past two months at the hospice place down the road from me. We went to visit her this morning. I'm glad we did.

February

The Winter Equivalent

The winter equivalent
To the summertime thing
Is one of isolation
And excessive comfort
The swaddling warmth
And the joyful seclusion
Completely at odds
To a July evening's fun
With friends out on the town

>February 22, 2025
>Lenox, Massachusetts

I wrote the title line in my phone's Notes app and it was something completely different at the time when I jotted it down. In the twelve hours since then, I've totally forgotten what I meant by it, so I did this instead. I'm happy how it came out.

Written while listening to "Finally Moving" by Pretty Lights.

The Shiver Of Winter

The shiver
Of winter
Is meant to
Shake us
Free of
Too much
Comfort
Is meant to
Wake us
Up to our
Chilly feet
Is meant to
Make us
Think of
Warmer
Days ahead

                February 22, 2025
                Lenox, Massachusetts

Written while listening to "Southpaw" by Morrissey.

If there were tarot cards of songs that were important to me through my life, this song would be The World. Ten minutes long, and note-perfect. It's the kind of song you can just get completely lost in.

Back in the mid 90s, in college, when I would make mixed tapes (and in the late 90s when I would make mixed cds [technology!]), my tape/cd with all of the BIG FEELING songs on it was called "Southpaw."

I'm getting all of the big stuff tonight. I've written a whole month's worth of poems in one night, so I'm calling it a night. Thank you for reading.

February

The Hunker Down

MARCH

The Hunker Down

Correctly Focused On This Shitty Car

Pausing to check my phone
In a parking lot
In the middle of
My little town
While parked beside
The local "Cyber Truck"
Seeing the passing people
All assuming they were alone
Focusing their rage
For all the national events
That we have no control over
By flipping off the monstrosity
Again and again and again
Nearly every person who passed
Gestured, or swore at it
Old people, young people, kids
The younger ones taking pictures
Of the rude finger pointing
While their parents were laughing
So much incredible hate
Correctly focused on this shitty car
That should have never been made
And much less, ever been bought

                March 9, 2025
                Lenox, Massachusetts

Written while listening to "Anxiety" by Doechii.

March

Exposure

Getting the word out
Often means
Displaying what
We don't want to show
So, we do what we do
Quietly. In the shadows
In hopes no one notices
But there comes a point
Where we have to stop
Worrying about what
Others may think
Of what we're doing
Of where we're going
And say loudly
And proudly
This is what I've done
If you don't like it:
Tough. I don't care.
If you do like it:
Great. Thank you.
And we all move on
But to get to this point
We have to be okay
With exposure
And exposing
The barest,
Innermost part
Of what we have

        March 9, 2025
        Lenox, Massachusetts

Written while listening to "God Knows" by Tunde Adebimpe.

The Hunker Down

Celebrate

Soon
We will all
Celebrate
By the light
Of the Teslas
Burning late
Into the night

                March 9, 2025
                Lenox, Massachusetts

Written while listening to "Forever and More" by Jaguar Sun.

March

Only Speaks Of Brightness And Activity

The longest day
Of the year so far
But this opens
The doorway
Entirely too wide
Saying it's okay
To be brighter
Longer, longer
Into the night
Paving way
For things like
Spring and summer
And yes, we're tired
Of this long winter
But we still don't want
To be the ones to give up
The quiet evenings
And the relaxing times
For this growing thing
Which only speaks
Of brightness and activity

    March 9, 2025
    Lenox, Massachusetts

Written while listening to "Projections" by Jose Junior.

The Carnivorous Intentions

In a small town
(By the salesmen's standards)
The pack of jackals
Went knocking
While assuming
And then hoping
This would be easy
Like shooting
Seals in an ice hole
Trying to get
Someone, anyone
To agree to talk
To agree to agree
To what they were selling
But not a single person
Would listen
Would open their doors
Would greet them
Would do anything
But curse them
Because they knew
The carnivorous intentions
Of the military-minded men
Who were only pretending
To play nice in this moment
But who publicly threatened
To invade and ensure
The entire country was ground
Deeply into submission
To satisfy the conquering intentions
Of the elderly madman

                      March 30, 2025
                      Lenox, Massachusetts

Pure insanity.

March

Written while listening to "All The Sad Young Men" by Spector.

Spring Cleaning

This is the time
For spring cleaning
Not for the house
Goodness no
Not for the yard
Haha, nope
But for the accounts
I follow on Instagram
Cutting and culling
Those that no longer
Do anything to serve me
Or are no longer posting.
The sharpened scythe
I am freely swinging
Is "Unsubscribe"
Over and over and over
Feeing myself
From the weight
Of the unnecessary

        March 30, 2025
        Lenox, Massachusetts

Written while listening to "Silence – Kryder Remix" by Delerium, Sarah McLachlan, and Kryder.

You're Not A Number

Waiting on hold
With a company
That does something
For my employer
Navigating their phone tree
Where they proudly say
"With us, you're not a number"
And then the irony
As the agent's first question is:
"What's your account number?"

                    March 30, 2025
                    Lenox, Massachusetts

Written while listening to "All That We See" by The Black Ryder.

The Hunker Down

The Not Quite Two Months

Reading a resume
From a person
Applying for a position
We currently have open
Listing Taco Bell
As a previous employer
Proudly stating
"I was the best cashier there"
Which would have been
A boastful claim
If they had been there
For longer than
The not quite
Two months
Their resume tells me
They had graced
Taco Bell with their presence

                March 30, 2025
                Lenox, Massachusetts

Written while listening to "Glory Box" by Portishead.

March

The Hunker Down

APRIL

I Am Doing This

Wanting to play a game
Like I would normally do
But not tonight
Instead of that
I am doing this
Following my intuition
And doing that thing
That I tend to do
Where I write write right

    April 14, 2025
    Lenox, Massachusetts

Written while listening to "Things We Do" by the insanely brilliant Kaki King.

April

Society's Canvas

It's like we're living in the times
Of a weird smash-up between
Harry Potter where we don't dare
To mention Voldemort's name
Because our devices are listening
And citizens are now being deported,
And the Handmaid's Tale
Scarily accurately depicting
What life is like in many of our states,
And the Hunger Games, showing
What we get to look forward to
In the very near future
And it makes me wonder
Why these authors
Had to lean so dystopian
Inadvertently painting
Society's canvas
Backdropping all our lives

        April 14, 2025
        Lenox, Massachusetts

Written while listening to "Automatic Buffalo" by The Sheila Divine.

Mid-April Snow

Mid-April snow
Is not appreciated
Or even welcomed
Yet, here it is
For the third time
Just this week

        April 14, 2025
        Lenox, Massachusetts

Written while listening to "La Contradiction" by Autour de Lucie.

April

I'll Wait For The Bus That Charges

The bus proudly wore a sign
Saying "RIDE FREE!"
But then I watched it
Flat out run a long red light
No thank you
I'll wait for the
Bus that charges
In hopes it's safer

    April 14, 2025
    Lenox, Massachusetts

Written while listening to "Bad Thing" by Miya Folick.

The Hunker Down

MAY

The Hunker Down

Everyone Can Stop

It feels like
It's been too long
To start here
In the middle
Of nowhere
Put stopping
For far too long
Is something
We tend to do
But starting
And continuing
The keeping going
Is the real key
Is the real test
Of the artist
Because everyone
Can stop easy peasy
But not all of us
Can overcome
The mind at rest
To resume creation
Once again

    May 20, 2025
    Lenox, Massachusetts

Written while listening to "Santa Fe" by Beirut.

May

The Lamp Lifted

There is no need
To mention how
Much worse things
Have gotten
As the bedrock
Has cracked
Splintered
And shattered
The lofty goal place
Is now shunned
Mocked and scorned
Worldwide
The lamp lifted
By the golden door
Has been extinguished
And the golden door
Has been moved
To a white house
With huge columns
Behind barbed wire
Protected from
The unwashed masses
And shared only with
The billionaire classes
Leaving this place
Shabby and tattered
Like a bankrupted casino
Once filled with luster
Now just sadly rusted
And the place
We used to live

        May 20, 2025
        Lenox, Massachusetts

The Hunker Down

Written while listening to "Impossible Weight" by Deep Sea Diver and Sharon Van Etten.

May

Trains About To Collide

Trains about to collide
Is how I'd describe
How things are currently
In this cursed country
Two giant locomotives
On the same track
Heading right at one another
But instead of braking
Trying to minimize casualties
The conductor is controlling
Both of them at once
Speeding speeding speeding
As fast as humanly possible
So someone else can swoop in
And buy the ruined remains
For pennies on the dollar
Which would be
In his words
"A big beautiful sale"

                May 20, 2025
                Lenox, Massachusetts

Written while listening to "Lithium" by The Polyphonic Spree.

The Hunker Down

Any Kind Of Lasting

The days are longer
At least they are
Only on paper
Because instead
Of demonstrating
Any kind of lasting
They are doing
Absolutely nothing
But speedily whizzing by
Faster than anyone
Could ever blink an eye

    May 31, 2025
    Lenox, Massachusetts

Written while listening to "Bags" by Clairo.

The Fuckwit Mating Call

The light turned red
So the first car stopped
Followed by the Harley
Followed by me
And, almost immediately,
The motorcycle started
Revving it's farting loudly
I couldn't figure out why
I mean, the light was red,
We couldn't go anywhere
I think it was just his attempt
At getting some kind of attention
An old man-child saying
"I'm bored! Look at me!
 I'm a toughie!"
Then I saw movement to my right
As another old man shuffled into view
After hearing the fuckwit mating call
He leaned to one side on the postal box
Took a drag off his cigarette
And gave an approving thumbs up
Which got the old man on the Harley
All kinds of worked-up horny
Making him rev, rev, rev that engine
And with each revving, his admirer
Gave a nod and another thumbs up
Each and every time
The motorized farting
Sprayed unnecessary noise pollution
All over every one of us
When the light turned green
And we started rolling
He didn't miss an opportunity
To rev, rev, rev some more
To let everyone know
How Harley he was…
Until he got totally smoked

The Hunker Down

By a kid on an electric scooter
Who, noiselessly, blurred on by
In the empty bicycle lane
Leaving the olde testosterone show
Completely in the dust

        May 31, 2025
        Lenox, Massachusetts

Seeing this made me laugh and laugh and laugh.

Written while listening to "Feriado" by Cornelio.

May

Until All The Seasons Blend

I meant to write about
The changing season
From woody winter
To budding spring
But I missed my chance
And now we're sitting
Deeply in full lushing
Late spring/early summer
With the exact moment
I meant to describe
Having happened
Several weeks ago
At the very least
And the worst part
Is that it'll happen
Again in a few months
And again a few months
Later, over and over
Until all the seasons blend
Into a permanent summer

    May 31, 2025
    Lenox, Massachusetts

Written while listening to "Plans" by Snowmine.

The Hunker Down

JUNE

Often Stunningly So

Just because
They're richer
Does not mean
They're smarter.
Usually and
Almost always
They're dumber –
Often stunningly so

                June 7, 2025
                Lenox, Massachusetts

Written while listening to "Phantom Of The Opera (live at the Hammersmith Odeon)" by Iron Maiden.

Holding Us Down

When will
All of this
Stupid shit
Radiating
From the
National level
That's
Holding us
Down
Holding us
Back
Finally be over
So humanity
Can finally resume
Continuing forward?

                June 7, 2025
                Lenox, Massachusetts

Written while listening to "Stomp Box" by They Might Be Giants.

Writer With A Capital W

When will it be official
When will it finally be real
When will I get
To call myself,
When will I be
Recognized as a
Writer with a capital W
Instead of the pretend version
I currently see myself as
At the moment and for
The past most of my life
Because it feels to me
That when I get
The recognition
That elevates the case
From a little "w"
To the big version
(The professional one)
Despite all of the words
Splattered across pages
Hundreds upon hundreds
In books, stories, essays,
And every other format
Where words and images
Are conveyed from me to you
When will it finally feel real?

      June 7, 2025
      Lenox, Massachusetts

An interesting conversation that Kari had with a friend yesterday who was questioning when she would feel like a real writer. Kari told her, "You already are. It's not for others to determine if you're a writer or not. You are a writer."

I get where she is coming from. I don't have anything official determining or approving my writing as "official" or me as a "poet" or an "author" other than the fact that I've published 18 books so far (19, if you're reading this). That makes me just as legitimate as anyone traditionally published. That's why I entitled my guided poetry journal *You Are A Poet* because if you write a poem, hey, guess what? You're a poet.

Written while listening to "Sideways" by The Sheila Divine.

It Was Truly Vegas

Overhearing a woman
Proudly bragging
While describing
A recent trip to a day spa
"It was truly Vegas"
Tells me two things:
One –
In reality, it was probably
Actually pretty terrible
Two –
She's clearly never
Visited Las Vegas
Not unless she has
And was trying to say
How gross it was
But I kinda doubt it

           June 7, 2025
           Lenox, Massachusetts

Written while listening to "Fool's Gold" by Dagny and BØRNS.

June

The Mere Mention

The mere mention
Of the place
Or the people
Suffering and
Trapped within
Is something akin
To the greatest sin
And don't you dare
To accurately describe
What's happening
Because they will
Break out the labels
To silence any
And all criticism
Of what they're doing

    June 7, 2025
    Lenox, Massachusetts

Written while listening to "Palestine" by Yann Tiersen.

The real crazy part is that I spent a solid four minutes mentally debating myself if I should even write that I was listening to that song (a song that has no words, just spelling the title over and over) out of genuine *fear* – that's how bad things are. I could have said I was listening to "In A Big Country" by Big Country, breathed easy and moved on with my evening.

Be The Light

Be the light
That shines
In these darkly
Regressive times

                    June 7, 2025
                    Lenox, Massachusetts

Written while listening to "Seasons (Waiting On You)" by Future Islands.

June

Every Possible Second You Can Afford To Give

Sometimes it's so hard
And nearly impossible
To shut out the world
Which is always always
Demanding attention
Every possible second
That you can afford to give
Until you can no longer
Afford to give even a moment
When you've been broken
And your bandwidth
Has been completely used up
But that's exactly when
You need to say enough
And shut it all out
Shut it all off
And take back
Your own mind
Take back
Your own thoughts
Spending them
On yourself
And no one else
Hunkering down
In blissful silence
Turning off the noise
And enjoying
Meditating
And recharging
Refilling yourself
With what you *need*
While shushing
What they're
Trying to sell you

        June 7, 2025
        Lenox, Massachusetts

The Hunker Down

Written while listening to "Anything You Synthesize" by The American Dollar.

This is one of my favorite songs. I don't listen to it nearly enough.

June

Mahoney

On a highway
We were driving
Alongside a truck
The kind that carries
Gas or propane
Or something similar
And, in huge letters,
It said, "MAHONEY"
And, for some reason,
My wife didn't think
It was Mahoney,
Like the last name
Of the person who owned
The gas or oil company
The truck belonged to,
But instead thought
The name was an abbreviation
For Massachusetts Honey
Like it belonged to
A Mass Honey association
And was full of honey
Which actually,
Is a possibility
I'd rather have
Stuck in my mind

        June 7, 2025
        Lenox, Massachusetts

Written while listening to "Chess" by Petite Noir.

Escalation

Escalation
Is never safe
Or comfortable
As the sum
Increases exponentially
With each raising
Of the stakes
With each notch
Resulting
In moving
Closer to the brink
We cannot pull back from

    June 14, 2025
    Lenox, Massachusetts

Written while listening to "Krack" by Soulwax and "Magick" by Ryan Adams & The Cardinals.

June

The Grayish Navy Is Just Enough

Nine o'clock
And the grayish navy
Is just enough
To backlight and
Silhouette the trees
Making me remember
A few months ago
When it was full dark
Just before five

        June 14, 2025
        Lenox, Massachusetts

Written while listening to "French Press" by Rolling Blackouts Coastal Fever.

The Hunker Down

Inspired By The Uninspired

Inspired by the uninspired
Moved to motivation
By the very ones
Who dream but don't do
Who plan big but won't act
Making me want
To work to leave my mark
Exactly where
They've left nothing

                June 14, 2025
                Lenox, Massachusetts

Written while listening to "Shoreline" by All Feels.

Everworse

Trying so hard
To avoid the news
Of this big day
Momentously important
On several fronts
For many different reasons
Because I know
Most everything
Will be terrible
And everworse
With society
Spiraling downward
Because I don't want
To see or know
To have a few
Blissful hours
Where I can pretend
Everything is fine
And ignore the fire
Torching the foundation
Of our country

                June 14, 2025
                Lenox, Massachusetts

Written while listening to "Changes" by Sugar.

A Whole New Perspective

Doing the thing
That brings the wings
Closer to the sun
Where the edges
Smoke and start
To smolder and burn
Making flying harder
And increasingly
And appealingly
Hazardous
With the danger
Not so much
Creeping in
But hitting hard
In all the wrong places
But lighting up
All the right places
As we spiral-dive
Into a whole new
Perspective
In these last
Few
Precious
Moments
We have left
Before becoming
One with the world
In a whole new way

    June 14, 2025
    Lenox, Massachusetts

Written while listening to "Spend The Money" by Fousheé and Lil Uzi Vert.

June

Man o man, I love this song. I just put it on and let the beat and feeling drive the words out of me.

I Think This Is The Way

Refusing to pay attention
Rejecting to be beaten
Just saying no to all of it –
I think this is the way
To take my mind
And my life back
From the never-ending assault
The hurricane of shit
Has dumped on the country
Over the past few months
Stay hunkered down
Keep me to myself
And focus on making
My immediate surroundings
As perfect and nice
As humanly possible

                      June 14, 2025
                      Lenox, Massachusetts

Written while listening to "Filibuster" by The Orange.

June

Sparsest Parade

Biggest baby
Sparsest parade
Simply because
He is hated

        June 14, 2025
        Lenox, Massachusetts

Hahahahahahahahahahahahahahahaha!

Written while listening to "In The End" by Think Of England.

Raising A Collective Finger

What if an infantile old man
Threw a fit and demanded
A massive military parade
The likes of which
Have never been seen here
The likes of which
Have only been seen
In those countries
Run by ruthless dictators
The kinds of which
He really admires
Thinking by throwing
This event he gets into
Their exclusive club
He gets to be
On their level
For a day, which,
Coincidentally
Is also his birthday

What if the crowds
The throngs, the masses
Never showed up?
What if, instead
They all protested
In their cities and towns
Tens of millions
In over two thousand locations
All raising a collective finger
In the baby's direct direction
All saying they've seen
Every dystopian movie series
Released in the past forty years
Where the people rise up
French Revolution-style
And definitively deal
With the oppressors

June

Once and for all
Bringing back
The long-awaited
Happily ever after

        June 14, 2025
        Lenox, Massachusetts

I told myself I would try to not write about what's been going on, but oops, sometimes it slips out.

Written while listening to "Good Morning" by The Dandy Warhols.

The Wake Of Make

Am I doing enough
Building and creating
To leave something
Behind in the wake
Of make I'm leaving
I think I probably am
But, to be honest,
I'm also not really sure
Which is why I keep going

                June 14, 2025
                Lenox, Massachusetts

Written while listening to "Fortnight (Taylor Swift cover)" by Call It Off.

June

A Cat Stopping By

The gentle brushing
Of long orange fur
Along the back
Of my bare legs
Done quickly in passing
While I'm writing
Is just a cat stopping by
To give me a hello

        June 14, 2025
        Lenox, Massachusetts

Written while listening to "Release The Squid (Box 6)" by The Deathray Davies.

Cahoots

It's seriously as if
My inspiration
And my playlists
Are in cahoots
Conspiring to make sure
I never stop writing
And I never go to bed
Despite my intentions
To stop writing
And go to bed

    June 14, 2025
    Lenox, Massachusetts

Written while listening to "God Is A Bullet – Live" by Concrete Blonde.

June

The Simpler Times

The simpler times
Were joyful
And peppy
Exceedingly light
And very happy

        June 14, 2025
        Lenox, Massachusetts

Written while listening to "Channel Z" by The B-52's.

A Poet's Dozen

A poet's dozen
Is that one extra
Added onto the day
The extra fries
Found loose in the bag
The bonus that delights
Nicely wrapping up
This long, wordy night

        June 14, 2025
        Lenox, Massachusetts

Written while listening to "Night Mail" by Public Service Broadcasting. This is one of my favorite songs I've discovered in the past year or so.

Closing The Loop

Living the life
Wanted and desired
By their parents
Not for their own
Wants and desires
But only done as a way
To honor their parents
Thinking that somehow
Completes the circle
Closing the loop
Despite not wanting
Or even caring
About the journey
Or the destination
Instead seeing it
As a means to an end

        June 14, 2025
        Lenox, Massachusetts

It's so hard to end an evening having written an odd number of poems (despite the title of the last one). Here's number fourteen. Goodnight.

Written while listening to "A Murder Of One" by Counting Crows.

The Last Bridge

The last bridge she burned was mine
Leaving the gulf between too wide
For either to cross over
From one to the other
Never again
Will I traverse across
At this point
Now, firmly
In my recent past
But with the embers
Still burning brightly
And the torch
Still in her hands
Safely across the void
That I no longer ever
Have to worry about
Now that I see that side
From a secure distance
It's not so appealing
Causing me to turn around
And head confidently
In a brand new direction

    June 25, 2025
    Lenox, Massachusetts

Written while listening to "Dernière Danse" by Indila.

Obliterated

The word used was
"Obliterated"
Which, in no way
Was correct
Or even remotely so
Except to describe
The credibility
Of the word's speaker
But that's not correct either
In any reality
Because
There wasn't any
Of that at all
To begin with

          June 25, 2025
          Lenox, Massachusetts

Written while listening to "Absinthe Party At The Fly Honey Warehouse" by Minus The Bear.

The Hunker Down

JULY

July

The Baby Bunny

The baby bunny in the yard
Is surprisingly very small
If I had a chocolate easter version
The small hollow kind
I could show you for scale
You might get the idea
Of exactly how small
We're talking about

        July 1, 2025
        Lenox, Massachusetts

Written while listening to "Seventeen" by Sjowgren.

The Hunker Down

Just Not Feeling It

The songs of one's youth
Are quickly remembered
Despite the decades since
The last listen, but
Often they completely lack
The swayish hold
They once did
Where you're singing along
But you're just not feeling it
While wondering why
You liked it so much back then

        July 1, 2025
        Lenox, Massachusetts

Written while listening to "Pets" by Porno For Pyros

I *really* liked this song in college, but now? Not so much. It's okay.

July

Let The Little Things

Every minute
Of
Every hour
Of
Every day
People
Everywhere
Let the little things
Become big things
That overwhelm
And consume
Their precious
Little time
With every tick
And every tock
Seconds slip by
Never to be
Lived again
And freely given
To what?
Something stupid

    July 1, 2025
    Lenox, Massachusetts

Written while listening to "Losfer Words (Iron Maiden cover) by Seis Cuerdas.

An Interesting Circle Of Events

It's an interesting circle of events
When the inspiration is drawn from
The wholly uninspired –
The person who is empty
And fully lacking
In the creativity
They once had
They were once filled with
They were once known for
And despite all of this
Sheer emptiness
They still, somehow
Manage to generate
A spark of something
In someone who
Happened into their orbit
At the exact right time
And managed to get
Exactly what they needed
To advance them along
Their own path
In a fruitful way

                July 1, 2025
                Lenox, Massachusetts

Written while listening to "Worn Me Down (EP version)" by Rachael Yamagata.

July

The Big Boom

I did not like
The big boom
Singular in sound
But deep and powerful
In volume and resonance
Too close for comfort
Hoping no more will follow
Especially if it was a shotgun
But looking at the calendar
It's more likely a backyard test
Of illegal, out-of-state fireworks
A quick test a few days before
The actual celebration day
To make sure it passes muster
In scaring the whole neighborhood

        July 1, 2025
        Lenox, Massachusetts

This just happened a few minutes ago. A singular big explosion that was maybe 150 to 300 feet (50 to 100 meters) away at about 9:15 pm.

I had originally written "passes mustard" which I greatly prefer, but I thought I should be correct with my word choice here.

Written while listening to "Mouthwash" by Kate Nash.

The Hunker Down

Nineteen Listens

A song I've listened to
For the past fifteen years
I don't know how
I discovered it
I've always liked it
But I guess not enough
To seek out and explore
Their other music
But it came on and I was
Fully into it
When I decided to tap
Onto their name on Spotify
And I saw the band
That made this great song
Only gets a mere
Nineteen listens per month
Which seems criminally low
So, I've increased that amount
By at least twenty five percent
To help make up for it

        July 1, 2025
        Lenox, Massachusetts

Written while listening to "Frog Logic" by The Preakness on repeat.

Inevitable Collapse

Inevitable collapse
Seems to be the aim
Of the gremlins
Both driving
And trying
To be crashing
The train
We're all on
Why?
As far as I can tell
The only reason
For the destruction
Is to be able to
Buy up the remains
For pennies
On the now
Worthless dollar

>July 19, 2025
>Lenox, Massachusetts

Written while listening to "Strange Overtones (David Byrne cover)" by We Barbarians.

Note: I think I wrote something very similar a few months ago. Sorry, I write a lot and sometimes similar topics and ideas resurface from time to time.

Someone Else's Job

Sure, I like the music
But a few albums
Is hardly a thing to pin
Your entire personality upon
It's like announcing
To the entire world
That your individuality
And your humanity
Equates only to
The physical output of
Someone else's job

                July 19, 2025
                Lenox, Massachusetts

Written while listening to "Goodbye Horses" by Venus Infers.

July

That's Exactly What They're Good At

Head down
Doing my thing
Under the radar
Like always
Trying not to
Attract attention
From the thugs
Who, suddenly,
Are in charge
Of everything
And lack ability
And awareness
To do their jobs
Even slightly
Or remotely properly –
Essentially
Just low-vibrational
Children
Without intelligence
Or any ability
For reasoning
Instead they were
Given a hammer
And told
To fuck shit up
And unfortunately
That's exactly
What they're good at

        July 19, 2025
        Lenox, Massachusetts

Written while listening to "Turn It Around" by Lucius.

So Easy To Imagine

It's so easy
To imagine
What "could've been"
Since we can simply
Look across an ocean
And see a near Utopia
Working correctly
Benefiting all
Who live there
Instead of here
Where the beneficiary
Is a handful
Of billionaires
In this system
That'll never change
And is nearing
Its inevitable end

    July 19, 2025
    Lenox, Massachusetts

Written while listening to "Losfer Words (Big 'Orra)" by Iron Maiden.

July

Tim Key

Tim Key
Is the only
Person I know
Who is absolutely
Full of ghee
He just eats
Massive scoops
Of the stuff
Right from the jar
With his hands
All the while
Staring directly
At you
Without breaking
Eye contact
Without stopping
His slurping
Without blinking
In a manner
That is described as
Uncomfortably
Horrifying

                July 19, 2025
                Lenox, Massachusetts

Apart from seeing him on *Taskmaster*, and reading his occasional poetry, I do not know Tim Key. However, I would like to think he would appreciate this.

Written while listening to "Nothing Matters" by The Last Dinner Party.

The Hunker Down

AUGUST

Mauvais Français Est Bon

J'ai une idee
Ou je parle
Dans le lange
Je sais a peine
Tout les temps
Juste parce que
Mauvais français
Tout les temps
Mauvais français
Est bon
Tout les temps
Dans ma tete
Dans tes oreilles

>   9 Août, 2025
>   Lenox, Massachusetts

I recently had an idea for a new YouTube channel called Mauvais Francais where I'd only speak in French. The trouble is I'm terrible at French. I took French for four years in high school (I got straight Ds, but I enjoyed it and stuck with it) and had a 1,000-day streak on Duolingo, gave it up, and re-started it and have over a year streak going now. Does that mean I know French? Non. Buuuuut, I thought if I started a YouTube channel of just me speaking terrible French a few times a week, maybe I'll get a little better at it.

Note: while I have the YouTube channel, and recorded a few videos for it, I have yet to actually start it. Hopefully soon(ish).

Écrit en écoutant "Stereophonic" par Midnight Fury.

It Can Always Get Worse

After the first time
I foolishly used to think
Well, it can't get any worse
But this time around
I know, without a doubt
That yes
It can always get worse

        August 9, 2025
        Lenox, Massachusetts

Written while listening to "The Sun" by The Naked And Famous.

The Volcano

The volcano
Spectacularly erupting
Forcefully spraying
Intensely hot lava
In a stunning fountain
Hundreds of meters
Shooting upward
Arcing impressively
And raining down
Covering the mountains
With the newest version
Of its future self
Layers upon layers
That came before
That'll continue
From this geyser now
And the others to come
Every one of them
A social media success
Making you pause
And nod impressively
At the power and forces
Involved in the spectacle

    August 9, 2025
    Lenox, Massachusetts

I saw an Instagram reel that showed a volcano in Hawaii that was spraying a massive fountain of bright orange lava probably 300 feet (100 meters!) in the air.

Written while listening to "The Moth & The Flame" by Les Deux Love Orchestra.

August

Pivoting Slightly

Still doing
What I used to do
(What I'm doing right now)
But changing just a little
Pivoting slightly
Incorporating a more
Artistic element
To the creative roster
Rounding it out
With drawn art
In addition to the poems,
And the novels,
And the movie script,
And the photography,
Making more of a symphony
Of creativity
Swirling the sounds
Instead of simply
Tooting the same note
Over and over
For years upon years

    August 9, 2025
    Lenox, Massachusetts

Written while listening to "Birdhouse In Your Soul (live)" by They Might Be Giants and "Two Feet Off The Ground" by The Dead Milkmen.

The Noise

Tuning out
The static
And the noise
Is a difficult thing
In these times
Where we're all
Plugged into
Everything
All the time
From the moment
We rise in the morning
To the moment we
Drift off to sleep
And beyond
For those who
Sleep while listening
To podcasts
Or other such media
The noise
Is ever-present
Like the elevated
Levels of stress
Within all of us
But
(but but but)
Tuning it out
Is getting more
Critically necessary
If we wish to function
In any normal capacity
So, please start now
By going for a walk
And leaving the noise and
The divisive devices behind

>August 9, 2025
>Lenox, Massachusetts

August

Just as I finished this poem, I received an alert on my monitor, my phone, and my watch saying that the washer machine had finished its cycle.

Written while listening to "To Know You" by Wild Nothing.

Monetized

After over two years
My numbers finally
Reached the number
Where YouTube says
"You're good enough"
And made me monetized
So I can start to share
In the advertising revenue
They make from my videos
After two and a half years
I've reached the point where
I have now made enough
In two weeks that would
Buy me something worth
Six dollars and eighteen cents

    August 9, 2025
    Lenox, Massachusetts

I've actually very excited about this. Sure, I'm making about $0.48 a day, but it's better than nothing…plus it feels good to be making money while I sleep.

Written while listening to "Getting There From Here (Miami Horror & Lazywax Remix)" by Poolside, Todd Edwards, Turbotito, Miami Horror, and Lazywax.

August

Purposely Not Sharing

Today we had a great day
Going out and doing stuff
And, despite the good day,
We were purposely not sharing
Any of it on social media
Because it was a day for us
To enjoy in our way
Not one
To crop, edit, and share
To untold strangers,
Bots, and AI scrapers
As a way to brag to others
That we're more exciting
Than we actually are

    August 9, 2025
    Lenox, Massachusetts

Today we got up early, grabbed some Dunks, and drove up to Williamstown where we went to the Clark Art Institute (clarkart.edu) and spent the morning walking through their amazing art galleries. After seeing the current exhibit on women artists in Great Britain from the mid 1800s to the early 1900s, Kari sat outside to enjoy an hour sitting in a very comfortable seat in the shade, looking at the reflecting pool and the big hill beyond while I walked through some of their other galleries, spending time with all of the Monets, Renoirs, Pissarros, Degas, and Singer Sargents.

The old me (like from just a few years ago or longer) would have been editing photos like mad and posting them as soon as I got home and been watching my likes like a hawk. That just seems like such a waste of time and energy now. Yeah, "let's give the richest people in the world more of my content for free so they can make money off of it." No thanks.

Written while listening to "It All Feels Right" by Washed Out.

The Smiles Frozen

After the passage of time
The fondness is what remains
Like the stone foundation
That seems to last in the mind
Which quickly forgets
Back then when the weeds
Were entwining and choking
The life out of everything else
Trying to grow in the same space
Leaving no air for anything
Making existing difficult
If not impossible
But we don't choose
To remember that part
Only the laughter
And the smiles
Frozen forever
In the photos
Strangely saved
Instead of burned
Or properly trashed
Like they should have been

    August 9, 2025
    Lenox, Massachusetts

Written while listening to "Would've, Could've, Should've" by Taylor Swift.

Last year Spotify said I was in the top 0.01% of all Taylor Swift listeners. This is probably my favorite song of hers.

August

Vanishing Into The Ravenous Past

Moving along
At a good clip
Is the way we
Go this time
Around the sun
In this life
Going fast
Like time
Is made of
Nothing
Solid or
Tangible
Or lasting
Here for
A moment
And then
It's gone
Vanishing
Into the
Ravenous
Past
Always
Consuming
The seconds
Before I can
Figure out
What to do
With them
Or use them
In some way
Which feels
Proper or right
And by the time
I spend too much
Time trying to
Figure out what
I want to do

The Hunker Down

The moment
Has passed
Completely
Leaving me
Behind in
The dust
Trying to
Pick up
The thoughts
And put them
Together
Into some kind
Of cohesive wish
Or, ideally, a plan
That I can BAM!
Execute with
Precision and
Determination
Each time
Every second
Without fail
Without failing
Success every
Time BAM!
Jumping from
This tick to
The next tock
Reacting so
Casually and
Confidently
Like a character
From a video game
Leaping from one
Ledge to another
Each being only
Wide enough to
Hold you for half
A second until
You have to react

August

And jump again
Over an abyss
Each and every
Time BAM!
Not wasting
A single moment
A single jump
But it's not
Sustainable
Because at
Some point
You have to
Stop
And rest
Pausing
To think
About what
You're doing
In this life
And do you
Really want
To keep living
Reacting like this
Every second
Every minute
Every hour
For every day
For decades
Upon decades
Until you slip
And trip
And miss
The ledge
Hitting wrong
Scrambling hard
To keep going
But it's too late
You reached
The point where

The Hunker Down

You can't
That moment
Where it all
Changed on you
And as you fall
You have those
Terrifying few
Seconds tumbling
Through the air
Supported by nothing
Where you are forced
To quickly face
The future
No matter
How brief
It is

        August 9, 2025
        Lenox, Massachusetts

This song started and I just wrote to it on repeat.

Written while listening to "Boy Girl (featuring Paul Conboy)" by Bomb The Bass.

This Is It

This is it
The last one
For the night
No more from me
No matter what
…
Unless
I'm enticed
By another
Great song
Stirring something
Deeply inside of me
Forcing me to abandon
The notion of going
To bed at an early hour
To catch up on sleep
Or something sensible
Until then
I'll be sitting here
Doing this thing
That I do
Writing until
The cat sits
On the keyboard
Stopping me
Fully and completely
For the evening

        August 9, 2025
        Lenox, Massachusetts

I wrote nine poems tonight before this one and then this Rachael Yamagata song came and I had to make it ten.

Written while listening to "Worn Me Down" by Rachael Yamagata.

The Hunker Down

If I could Tell My Past Self One Thing

If I could tell
My past self one thing
I would say nothing
Because they need
To learn life lessons
On their own
For themselves.

Actually,
Screw that.

I'd go back
And tell the me
From 2009
Who first became aware
Of Bitcoin back when
It was nine dollars each
To buy as many as possible
Because I'd be
A billionaire now

        August 16, 2025
        Lenox, Massachusetts

Written while listening to "Voià" by Barbara Pravi.

Note while editing: Apparently I seem to be cranky with other billionaires but it's A-okay if it were me. (eyeroll emoji.)

August

I Need To Fold This Bag Of Laundry

I need to fold this bag of laundry
Sitting by my side
But instead I'm here, writing
When I should be folding
Preventing the wrinkles
That are happily forming
On all of my work clothes
Knowing that I will never
Get around to ironing
But, at the moment
I don't really care
I'm plenty happy doing this

           August 16, 2025
           Lenox, Massachusetts

Written while listening to "It's Not Enough" by Heaven.

Dreaming Of A Place

Dreaming of a place
Never visited
Only pictured
In the mind
Wanting to be
More than anything
Is the way
It sometimes goes
For no reason
That can be determined
Or discerned
But here we are
Thinking the thoughts
Just the same

    August 17, 2025
    Lenox, Massachusetts

Written while listening to "California Dreamin'" by The Mamas & The Papas.

August

Ascending

The spirit ascending
From the old and done
To the never-ending
Ancient and broken
Changing to pure energy
Lighter than air
Recharging fully
To the forgotten levels
While surrounded
By so many
Who have gone before
Congratulating this
Special homecoming
For the one who lived
The lemon life

           August 17, 2025
           Lenox, Massachusetts

Written while listening to "Moonwalk Away" by Goldfish.

A Favorite

A favorite
Of mine
Hidden in
Among the
Favorites
Of others
On this
Record

>August 17, 2025
>Lenox, Massachusetts

Written while listening to "Flash Of The Blade" by Iron Maiden.

I used to be able to play this on guitar (not the whole thing, just the main bit).

August

The Pungent Crispness

The pungent crispness
Hanging lightly in the air
Making me think
"Ugh, who is smoking"
But realizing
No one here smokes
That, or anything,
And no one lives
Close enough
To be able to smell that
From a neighbor
Which means
That it's actually
From a skunk
But since it's daytime
That means there's one
Under my feet
Under the back deck
Having a nap
Or, there's one
Wandering around
And possibly rabid
Since they're nocturnal
Either way
I finish what I'm doing
And head back inside
Just in case

        August 17, 2025
        Lenox, Massachusetts

Written while listening to "Oobleck" by Kaki King.

Did The Chair Topple?

Did the chair topple?
No, it did not
But it almost did
When I tried to scooch
Forward just a bit
Giving me that ounce
Of instability
Widening the eyes
For a fraction
Of a moment
Until everything
Stabilized somewhat
And settled properly

        August 27, 2025
        Lenox, Massachusetts

Written while listening to "Flagpole Sitta" (Harvey Danger cover) by MS MR.

August

Rise Above The Standard Couchiness

The feeling of determination
Filling my insides
Invincibly warm
Like a shot of alcohol
Or maybe three
Giving me that kick
Pushing me forward
Making me rise above
The standard couchiness
That tends to dominate
The daily routine
But not now
With this inside me
It feels like I can
Accomplish anything
Pushing forward
With no stopping
Keeping going
Endlessly

>   August 27, 2025
>   Lenox, Massachusetts

Written while listening to "Live Forever – Live at Glastonbury '95" by Oasis.

I don't give two hoots about Oasis, but dang this version of this song is proper lush.

The Summer Is Over

The summer is over
And done with officially
I know that the
Calendar says differently
That it's got
Another whole month
But it's wrong
When the leaves start
Crisping
And the tourists start
Leaving
And the festivals stop
Running
And the pop ups start
Closing
Down down down
Laying off
The seasonal help
And all the prices start
Dropping
For those who live here
When the parking
Becomes plentiful
Once again
Is really when
The summer is over

        August 27, 2025
        Lenox, Massachusetts

Written while listening to "The Fall" by Rhye.

August

Trying To Raise My Vibration

Trying
To raise
My vibration
Trying
To rise above
All the shit
We've been
Swimming in
Trying not
To get stuck
Thinking about
Where we are
And where
We're heading –
Trying to rise
Above all of that
Because, at some point
All of this will end
History shows
It always does
So, until then,
I choose to protect
My energy
And use it
To lift up others
Whenever possible

        August 27, 2025
        Lenox, Massachusetts

If you get too stuck in the daily awfulness, you'll either shrivel and die, or become a "low person" like them.

Written while listening to "Swimming" by Flawed Mangoes.

The Hunker Down

SEPTEMBER

The Past Is Hungry

The past
Is hungry
And rarely
Funny
No matter
How much
You want
To go there
Don't ever
Do that
Because
You may
Never ever
Come back

                September 3, 2025
                Lenox, Massachusetts

I just put on this song and wrote to it. This also feels a little familiar, like I might have written something very similar to this either this year or last year.

Written while listening to "Cut" by The Cure

September

Trying To Drown Out Their Voices

Imagine being so afraid
Of what a group of women
At a press conference
Have to say
That you will waste
Millions of dollars
Ordering military planes
To fly overhead
Over and over
Trying to drown out
Their voices

    September 3, 2025
    Lenox, Massachusetts

Written while listening to "Moonchild" by Iron Maiden.

Flourishes In Shadows

Satisfaction
Is not found
Easily in this
Backward place
The concept
Of which is
Apparently
Obviously
Foreign
In nature
And only
Flourishes
In shadows

                  September 3, 2025
                  Lenox, Massachusetts

Written while listening to "I Love You All The Time" by OH NO OH MY.

September

The Longing Twang

The longing twang
Of the slide guitar
Should have told you
To keep drinking
While thinking
About the things
You've been avoiding

        September 3, 2025
        Lenox, Massachusetts

Written while listening to "Blow" by Lincoln.

The self-titled (and only) album by Lincoln (released in 1997) is a true masterpiece. I was fortunate enough to have seen them in concert (twice!) opening for They Might Be Giants, who ended up stealing two of their band members.

The Hunker Down

OCTOBER

Sans Plans

Sans plans
But here I am
Writing this
Like a warm-up
Exercise
Breaking in
The fingers
Un-mushing
The mind
Getting settled in
For resuming
The thing I do
That I haven't done
In much too long

        October 12, 2025
        Lenox, Massachusetts

Written while listening to "The Fate Of Ophelia" by Taylor Swift.

October

Moving To My Moon Line

Moving to my moon line
Where this life I'm in
Should change radically
And blow wide open

        October 12, 2025
        Lenox, Massachusetts

Had a wonderful astrocartography session recently that really opened my eyes and bombarded me with coincidences.

Written while listening to "Deli" by Delorean.

Concrete Steps

Before it was
Just thinking
But there was
A lot of that
Now, it seems
Things are happening
Steps are being made
Real hardy concrete steps
Not the cheapy plastic kind
The kinds of movement
You can't step back from
Honest and true commitment
Pushing you forward
Toward that goal
You once dreamed of
But now it seems
A whole lot more real
And not all that far
Down the road
In the grand scheme of things
It's real and it's happening
Because it's been set in motion
And it's approaching
Due to the movement
And direction you're heading on

        October 12, 2025
        Lenox, Massachusetts

Written while listening to "Drunk On A Rhythm" by Gothic Tropic.

The Only Difference Is You

The huge city
You are visiting,
Living and flowing
Would be doing
The exact same thing
If you were here
Or if you were not
These people around you
Would still be here
Doing this exact thing
At this exact time
The only difference is you
Being a witness to it all

          October 12, 2025
          Lenox, Massachusetts

Written while listening to "Respire Encore" by Clara Luciani.

The Prize Pony

The prize pony
Is all aloney
In the stable
Of your cluttered mind
And, when offered hay,
It says "Neigh"
And resumes laying down
A sick bass line
On the guitar
I didn't know it had
Or even knew
It knew how to play

                October 18, 2025
                Lenox, Massachusetts

Written while listening to "Southern Point" by Grizzly Bear.

October

Post Something

If you post something
On an online platform
And no one interacts
Or responds to it
And you post again,
And again, asking questions
As if you don't have
Access to the Googles
Like the rest of us do,
Or you try to start conversations
Based around the divisive subjects
Of wanting coffee in the morning
Or hating Mondays
Are you being clever,
Or are you instead being
Someone I am now blocking
For being absurdly annoying

                October 18, 2025
                Lenox, Massachusetts

Written while listening to "Do Your Worst" by Vagabon.

The Hunker Down

Get Off Our Couches

Yes, they have the money
But we have the people
And, in the end,
It honestly looks like
We might finally be
Motivated enough
By the obscene injustices
To get off our couches
And finally do something

                    October 18, 2025
                    Lenox, Massachusetts

Written while listening to "Krack" by Soulwax.

The Burger King Crown

The Burger King crown
Upon the greasy head
Of the ratings-obsessed liar
Does not convey any powers,
Autocratic or plenary,
Despotic, or dictatorial,
No matter the deranged beliefs
Of the one wearing it
Thinking they are a king
When, in fact,
They rule absolutely nothing

        October 18, 2025
        Lenox, Massachusetts

Written while listening to "In Remote Part / Scottish Fiction" by Idlewild.

The Hunker Down

NOVEMBER

The Hunker Down

Incredibly Rich

The multitudes
Who easily believe
That the stream of lies
Are actually truths
Are incredibly rich
In nothing
But ignorance

        November 22, 2025
        Lenox, Massachusetts

Written while listening to "Weakness" by Dear Leader

November

Stretching The Mind

Stretching
The mind
Is exactly
The kind
Of fitness
That's fallen
Out of favor
Among pretty
Much everyone

        November 22, 2025
        Lenox, Massachusetts

Written while listening to "I Should Be Allowed To Think" by They Might Be Giants.

The Hunker Down

Filtered

Words now
Must be
Filtered,
Thoughts
Should be
Kept within,
Anything
Contradicting
The top-down
Prevailing decree
Needs to be
Silent, quieted,
Never spoken
Because betraying
Oneself will only
Ensure the troops
Will kick in your doors,
Smash your windows,
Cuff you, lock you up,
Send you to prison
In a far-off country
Never to be heard from again

        November 22, 2025
        Lenox, Massachusetts

Written while listening to "In Remote Part/Scottish Fiction" by Idlewild.

November

The Calendar Blinks

Time
Moves
Much
Too quickly
To handle
Or even to
Get a chance
To grab onto
So slippery
When you think
"Here's where I am"
But the calendar blinks
And now it's a month later
And your to-do list
Is twice as long
With nothing having
Gotten done

        November 22, 2025
        Lenox, Massachusetts

Written while listening to "Drunk On A Rhythm" by Gothic Tropic.

Mostly Full Of Red Lights

Why is it
That I feel stuck
Always in a place
Of waiting
Like my life
Is mostly full
Of red lights
With me sitting
In the driver's seat
Raring and ready
But going nowhere
For an extended time
Maybe this is
A life lesson
That I need to learn
That I need to get past
Once and for all
Finally figure out my shit
And step fully
Into my dreams
Once and for all

>November 22, 2025
>Lenox, Massachusetts

Written while listening to "Pursuit of Happiness" by Lissie.

November

Fast Forward

When I press
Fast forward
From this moment
And move ahead
To see the difference
To know that
The familiar
Will be gone
Utterly and completely
To know everything
Has been left behind
In an inaccessible place
In order to do what, exactly?
Satisfy a hunch?
A geographical itch?
To put myself deeply
Inside my astrocartography
To the point where
Nothing will be recognizable
But supposedly
Everything will be
As it should?
Is it worth it?
I don't know
So much time
Thinking about this
But I still don't know

    November 22, 2025
    Lenox, Massachusetts

Written while listening to "Old Town Blues" by Boy & Bear.

The Hunker Down

Their Charm

How come
Hogwarts
Changes so much
From one movie
To another
With no rhyme or reason
The castle grows
New towers
New wings
That have
"Always been there"
For hundreds of years
But only in the current film
But by the next one
It's different again
And somehow
No one notices
Well I did
And their charm
Or spell or whatever
Didn't work on me

        November 22, 2025
        Lenox, Massachusetts

Written while listening to "There Is A Light That Never Goes Out" by the Dum Dum Girls.

November

Just Knowing

Sometimes
Just knowing
Is enough
To give the
Motivation
To get through
The time
You're in

        November 22, 2025
        Lenox, Massachusetts

Trusting one's intuition is important.

Written while listening to "High Hopes" by Panic! At the Disco.

Earworm

This damn
Earworm
Is stuck
Hopelessly
In my mind
Replaying
Constantly
And honestly
I don't mind

                November, 22, 2025
                Lenox, Massachusetts

Written while listening to "Golden" by HUNTR/X.

November

Gravy

I think I may have
Misheard the lyrics
Because I don't think
Taylor Swift sings
"You dug me out
 Of my gravy"
On that new song of hers
Or, maybe she did,
I don't know
She could really love
Thanksgiving dinner
And goes really overboard
With the gravy-portion
Of it all

        November 22, 2025
        Lenox, Massachusetts

Written while listening to "The Fate of Ophelia (Loud Luxury Remix)" by Taylor Swift.

The Hunker Down

DECEMBER

All Banned

Books
Beliefs
Countries of origin
Skin colors
Religions
Liberties
All banned
And purposely
Oppressed
And removed
From the view
Of the ruling class
Who are ignorant
That government
Is FOR the people
And not against
Those it should
Be serving

December 11, 2025
Lenox, Massachusetts

Written while listening to "Maroon" by Taylor Swift.

December

When The Weight

When the weight
Of the stress
Presses down
Threatening to
Grind you
Into the ground
Stop.
Breathe.
Take a moment
To think
Will this matter
In twenty years?
If the answer is no
Let the worries
Fall from your shoulders
And get going
Doing something
More pleasant and fun

    December 11, 2025
    Lenox, Massachusetts

Written while listening to "Je Veux" by ZAZ.

The Purpose Of The Year

The purpose of the year
Was to do the hunker down
Was I successful?
No, not at all
I had hoped
I would eschew
The terrible news
And avoid
Intense negativity
By staying to myself
And only going out
When it was
Truly necessary
But that didn't work out
Like I had planned
But
(but but but)
It seems like
2026 is gearing up
To be like 2025
But a hundred times
More hardcore
So, maybe
Just maybe
I'll get my chance
In the year after
The hunker down
Was initially intended

    December 11, 2025
    Lenox, Massachusetts

Written while listening to "Robot Rock/Oh Yeah (live)" by Daft Punk.

December

Face-Forward

Jealousy
Aimed at
Those who
Are living
The carefree
And cheery
Life I wish
Was the
Version of me
That presented
Face-forward
And out there
Without a care
What anyone
Could ever think
The kind of life
Where you do
Exactly as you
Desire and please
Where every moment
Is the highest quality
Of high-vibrational
Living
Actual honest-to-goodness
Living

        December 11, 2025
        Lenox, Massachusetts

Written while listening to "Habits" by Tove Lo.

The Hunker Down

Icing Over

It snowed once
And got cold
Icing over
The ground
And surfaces
Making venturing
Outside something
No one wants
To do if they
Don't have to

                December 11, 2025
                Lenox, Massachusetts

Written while listening to "Diet Pepsi" by Addison Rae.

December

The Flames Of The Endgame

What is the endgame?
It's not like they can
Just remove millions
And dismantle
The entirety
Of our society.

"It's not like that
 Could ever happen here,"
They thought,
Ninety years ago
And it did happen
Humanity has been
On this train before
One that needs
To stop or be
Derailed before
We reach the flames
Of the endgame
We're racing toward

        December 11, 2025
        Lenox, Massachusetts

Written while listening to "You're Gonna Need Someone On Your Side (live)" by Morrissey and "Bag Of Bones" by Lord Huron.

It Tastes Like Shapes

It tastes like shapes
The kind that stand out
The kind that prick
And nearly puncture
Leaving the taste,
Crimson red,
Metal-like, and lingering
Like an exclamation point
Lasting in a way
That is unwanted
And a setting up
For craved re-match
Crazy for thinking
This way but unable
To avoid the oncoming
Collision with the next
Instance of the occurrence
Two trains heading
Directly at one another
Unable to swerve
Unable to stop in time
To prevent the inevitable
So instead, we floor it,
Heading for the impact
Bracing for everything
We ever dreamed facing
Because in an instant
There will be no more

December 21, 2025
Lenox, Massachusetts

Written while listening to "Rabbit Hole" by Cherry Glazerr on repeat.

December

What We Are Capable Of

What we are capable of
Is wonderful
But what we actually do
Is pitiful
Surrendering to our fears
Instead of building
Our confidences
Which is something
We need to get working on
Right away
Without delay
Starting by
Ignoring the low people
Who seek to bring you
And everyone else down
To their level in the dirt
Rise above their
Negativity
Lift yourself up above
The density
They seek to trap you in;
Float high and free
Feeling the warmth
Of the sun and the light
And the new perspective
The altitude gives you
And from this place
Start to create
The life you want
The life you deserve

    December 21, 2025
    Lenox, Massachusetts

Written while listening to "L'escalier" by The Pirouettes.

The Ceiling

The ceiling
Limits expansion
Which is why
All the mansions
Have such high walls
To let the occupants know
Nothing limits them at all
So they keep doing what
They want to do whenever
While the rest of us stay
Content in our places
Which hold us down
With our nine feet (or less)
Because honestly, it's all
We've been allowed to know
But when we can experience
And see for ourselves
Is when we get a taste
Of how things could be
Turning the gears in our minds
And start planning
For a better future
Someday
Somehow

December 21, 2025
Lenox, Massachusetts

Written while listening to "Hold On, Hold On" by Neko Case and "Close To Me" by Fred Avril.

December

The Beautiful Thing

The beautiful thing
About collections like this
Is that I am the one who decides
When the year starts
And when it ends
The power of creation
The content within
The ability to close a chapter
And to start anew
All given from me to you
Year-in
Year-out
And this one
Despite its slight ups
And terrifying downs
Is hereby over
But!
(there's always a but)
I will be back
In another year
Changed wholeheartedly
By what life has in store
Full of adventures
Never considered
Until I find myself
In the midst of them

        December 21, 2025
        Lenox, Massachusetts

Thank you for reading and coming along on my journey with me. I appreciate you.

Written while listening to "Schaerbeek Love (Mondial Toboggan Remix) by Ecran Total.

The Hunker Down

IF YOU ENJOYED THIS COLLECTION

Please consider rating it at Amazon.com. As an independent author, having people review my works is critical in helping to increase my exposure and letting new people discover books like this. Thank you!

WRITTEN BY ERIC NIXON

The Hunker Down – 2025 poetry collection
The Comfortable In-Between – 2024 poetry collection
When Time Was Stable – 2023 poetry collection
Indestructible – 2022 poetry collection
The Length Of A Second – 2021 poetry collection
The Year That Aged Us – 2020 poetry collection
You Are A Poet – guided poetry journal
Caught In Pause – 2019 poetry collection
Equidistant – 2018 poetry collection
The Cupcake – 2017 poetry collection
2492: Attack Of The Ancient Cyborg – science fiction novel
The Ocean Above – 2016 poetry collection
Cascadia's Fault – 2015 poetry collection
The Taborist – 2014 poetry collection
The Entire Universe – 2013 poetry collection
Trying Not To Blink – 2012 poetry collection
Lost In Thought – poetry collection
Emily Dickinson – Superhero: Vol. 1 – historical fiction novel
Incident On The Hennepin – a short story set in *2492*
Plenty Of Time – a short story
Retribution On A Jetpack – a short story set in *2492*
Anything But Dreams – poetry collection

Available at Amazon.com/author/ericnixon

ABOUT THE AUTHOR

Eric Nixon is a poet and author who has written sixteen poetry collections, a guided poetry journal, several short stories, and two novels – *2492: Attack Of The Ancient Cyborg* and *Emily Dickinson, Superhero: Vol. 1*. Eric lives in the Berkshires of western Massachusetts with his author wife, Kari Chapin Nixon.

The Hunker Down

www.ingramcontent.com/pod-product-compliance
Lightning Source LLC
Chambersburg PA
CBHW071705090426
42738CB00009B/1673